Six Cubs

By Jamie Daniels

Illustrated by Joe Kulka

Target Skill Short *Uu*/u/

Scott Foresman
is an imprint of

Six fat cubs are in a den.

Get up cubs!

Six fat cubs spot ten bees.

Six fat cubs run to the tree.

4

Six fat cubs jump up the tree.

Six fat cubs look at it.

Six fat cubs grab it.

Six fat cubs run!

Run to the den fast, fat cubs.